RECORDED VERSIONS GUITAR

AUTHENTIC TRANSCRIPTIONS
WITH NOTES AND TABLATURE

BEST OF
alex de grassi

T0083947

Cover photo by ANDREW deLORY. All Rights Reserved

ISBN-13: 978-1-4234-0724-9
ISBN-10: 1-4234-0724-5

HAL•LEONARD® CORPORATION

7777 W. BLUEMOUND RD. P.O. BOX 13819 MILWAUKEE, WI 53213

Visit Hal Leonard Online at
www.halleonard.com

ACKNOWLEDGEMENTS

Thanks to the staff at Hal Leonard for their patience and guidance. A big thanks to Andrew DuBrock for helping me edit and complete the transcriptions. Thanks to Will Ackerman and Anne Kasten for facilitating the publication of much of this music. Many thanks to John Stropes and John Wunsch for their encouragement and deep commitment to promoting fingerstyle guitar. Thanks to my wife Alison for proofreading, care, and feeding. And thanks to Jeff Titus and the many other players and students for pushing me to dig deeper into the process.

–Alex de Grassi

Here, finally, is the follow-up to my previous Hal Leonard book *Alex de Grassi: Guitar Collection* published in 1991. In the preface to that book, I tried to offer insights to my approach to composing and performing music for solo steel-string guitar. Much of what I wrote then still holds true but, in the intervening years, I have continued to make new discoveries and to learn from other players and composers, both past and present. Consequently, in this preface, I hope to expand on those earlier thoughts and integrate some of what's new. While all the pieces in this book were composed prior to 1992, these insights apply to both the very early pieces as well as those composed towards the end of that period.

I've always believed that a successful solo guitar composition or arrangement depends on the orchestration of voices or lines within the music. That is to say, if a composition contains two or more voices and the voices are differentiated using devices such as dynamics, timbre, and "call and response," then it's possible to hear a dialogue within the music in the form of interplay between those voices. The ability of the player to draw out these voices and create the tension and resolution in that interplay is what ultimately makes for a successful performance of the composition. It's not unlike how a director works with actors to shape characters and bring a successful drama to the stage. Without the tension and resolution, the music, like the play, might fall flat.

So what are the primary devices employed in the composition and performance of the pieces contained in this book? In the preface to my 1991 Hal Leonard book, I stressed the importance of utilizing accents to create a "hierarchy of accents" as a means of giving more depth to the music and creating a "three-dimensional sound." That approach relies heavily on the ability of the player to not only pay close attention to dynamics from one passage to another, but also to employ dynamics by way of constantly choosing the right amount of pressure or "accent" for a succession of notes that occur within an arpeggio or a short passage. I use the analogy of the photography term "depth of field" to suggest that some notes in any given passage may be played forcefully as if in the foreground, while other, adjacent notes might be played with less force, or in the middle ground, while others are played so softly that they blend into the background.

I still feel this approach lies at the heart of my music and my way of playing. But it was particularly true with some of my earliest compositions, as I relied on this to the exclusion of other very useful techniques—most notably string-stopping. Somewhat seduced by the special resonance that alternate tunings provide, I conceived and played those pieces somewhat like a pianist whose foot is always on the sustain pedal. Consequently, my means of bringing interplay and a three-dimensional sound to the performance was entirely dependant on dynamics and the hierarchy of accents method. Since then, I've discovered and have begun to integrate that method with string-stopping, or damping.

The late Michael Hedges was a master of string-stopping, and the technique was an integral part of both his compositions and performances. The technique has been used to some extent by classical guitarists, bass players, and in various steel-string styles such as blues and various folk music, but Michael was at the forefront of systematically utilizing the technique in what might now be called the solo steel-string guitar genre. The ability to precisely control the duration of notes is a powerful tool in expressing the interplay between musical lines and sonic textures.

In this collection, you will find that transcriptions such as "Sleeping Lady" and "Turning Back" rely primarily on the hierarchy of accents method, while others like "Short Order" and "Blue Trout" also employ string-stopping. Tablature is essential for learning all these pieces as they are in alternate tunings. However, the system of tablature used in this book merely tells the player where the notes are played on the fingerboard. To really understand the note durations and be able to employ string-stopping techniques, it is necessary to study the standard notation. String-stopping sometimes requires lifting the fingerboard hand partially or completely off the strings; at other times it will require stopping the string with the picking fingers.

Among the other devices that can be used to good effect is timbre or tone color. By contrasting the metallic sound produced near the bridge with the warm or darker sound produced by playing in front of the sound hole, the music can take on a new dimension. I have made timbre markings in a few places, but the player should always experiment. Some of the extended techniques utilized in these pieces also produce new timbres or sonic textures. For example, an array of overtones is produced by the percussive slapping of strings in "Blue Trout."

Another device is articulation. The use of vibrato, chord vibrato ("Deep at Night"), slides, bends, pizzicato, or muted notes ("Turning: Turning Back") is sometimes noted where it is essential to the music, but these are devices that the player should explore even when not marked. By constantly playing with and combining articulations in a musical phrase, the player can enhance the overall shape of the line. The notes should always be moving and changing shape over time.

– Alex de Grassi

BLOOD & JASMINE

This piece has many short sections with slightly con-voluted reiterations of the original theme. There's a double hammer-on to the chord in the third measure that needs to be hammered-on forcefully enough to be heard. After the spacious rubato A section, it goes relentlessly into time at letter B until a fermata at the end of letter F on page 15. Using the right hand fingerings indicated will help make the piece flow. Accenting the harmonics in letter D will carry the syncopated rhythm.

BLUE TROUT

Many parts of this piece should be played percus-sively. Starting with the last eighth note in measure 2, the series of bass notes should be slapped with the side of the thumb, pushing the strings against the frets and making a percussive sound. The chord that begins the measure before letter C is played by brushing the right hand index finger from the top to bottom string and releasing the left hand fingers immediately after the strings they are fretting are plucked. A long sequence of slapped chords (right index finger) against slapped bass, that incorpo-rates both harmonics and non-harmonics, begins at letter C. By experimenting with moving the right hand while playing this section, many other "un-notated" harmonics and overtones can be produced to good effect.

BRIGHT SKY

This piece shows the influence of Brazilian samba and is accordingly written in 2/4. Throughout this piece, and especially in the introduction and the end section, varying the right hand position gradually over the repetitive pattern creates movement and a sense of development. The melody begins at mea-sure 21 and is played in the bass using the thumb. This allows the rhythmic pattern to continue in the upper voices as slowly changing chord harmonies are played with the fingers. The pattern is somewhat broken by a new melody played in the upper voice beginning at measure 75. The original pattern resumes, played even more staccato at measure 113 and building on subtle variations in the harmon-ic progression. A fast run occurs at measure 71 as well at the end of the piece; these require some pre-cision.

CUMULUS

This piece has influences of both jazz and Brazilian folk music. The rubato introduction is written in 3/4 time, but should be played quite freely without too much regard for the time signature. The next section (letter B), while feeling some influence of Brazilian rhythms, is written in 4/4 as it has an underlying swing feel. At letter C the time signature changes (as does the tempo) to 2/4 because from here out, the piece really does feel more like a samba rhythm, and samba is typically written in 2/4. It's very impor-tant in this section to emphasize the upbeat six-teenth notes and to de-emphasize the sixteenth notes that are played on the downbeat (they should be played very lightly) on the first one and a half measures of the two measure phrase. On the last beat of the second measure of the phrase, the accent turns around. Achieving this feel will carry the piece to the end.

Deep at Night

This is a ballad with some unusual harmonies. It should be played very slowly with ample use of vibrato, dynamics, and variations in timbre. Using vibrato on whole chords and triads helps create a floating sensation. The time starts somewhat rubato and gradually becomes more steady at measure 13, but there's room for stretching the time a bit, especially in the passage beginning at measure 46. The tempo picks up at measure 82 in letter D, builds momentum, and then the rest of the piece is played in straight time.

Klamath

Klamath is the name of a mountain wilderness area and for the Native Americans who have inhabited it in northern California and southern Oregon. Like the area, this piece has a rugged contour with many sudden, precipitous changes and the compositional structure is a bit wild and unpredictable. Letter A can be played by taking liberties with the time, and creating short pauses. The tempo becomes more regular at measure 34 but is still subject. The pitch bend in measures 3 and 114 should go up and down slowly and evenly over the duration of the measure.

Short Order

This piece is short and fast. It starts with an unaccompanied bass line with some double stops. Snapping the strings back on to the fingerboard gives this section a little more character. At letter B the melody begins, leading triads that sound a little like a horn section. Keeping the note durations discrete will help differentiate the chords and the melody from the bass line. Keeping the anticipations precise also helps define the music. At letter C, pluck the harmonics with force and let them ring through while playing the bass line below to contrast the two parts.

Sleeping Lady

A very linear piece with a meditative quality, "Sleeping Lady" employs a lot of open, droning strings. For these reasons, it's important to emphasize the melody notes and make them jump out from the background. Using vibrato and varying the timbre and dynamics help give the piece definition and help make the rhythm breathe.

Turning: Turning Back

This piece was originally recorded as two separate pieces: "Turning," and "Turning Back." "Turning Back" is really an extension of the piece "Turning," and features a long double-time section starting at letter C that is improvised off a simple three beat pattern. The pattern takes on the character of a hand drum when the unison notes played on adjacent strings are articulated differently from each other. At letter D, if the fretted A on the 3rd string is played staccato, or even pizzicato (finger directly on the fret), and the fretted A on the fourth string is played with vibrato, those two textures can be played off the twangy, sustained open 2nd string A. Then at measure 160, add the deepness of the lower octave A on the fifth string played on the downbeat of the pattern. This is much like the way a hand drummer plays different areas of the skin with open and closed strokes, and it adds a vital dimension to the long middle section.

from *Turning: Turning Back*

Blood & Jasmine

By Alex de Grassi

Gtr. 1, Tuning: (low to high) D-A-D-E-A-D

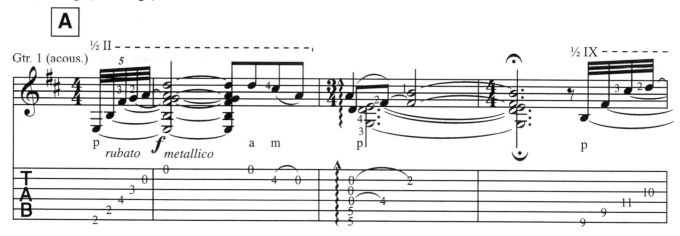

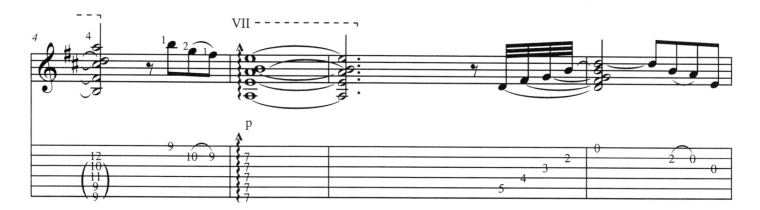

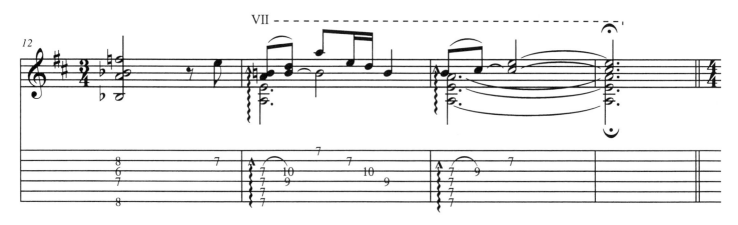

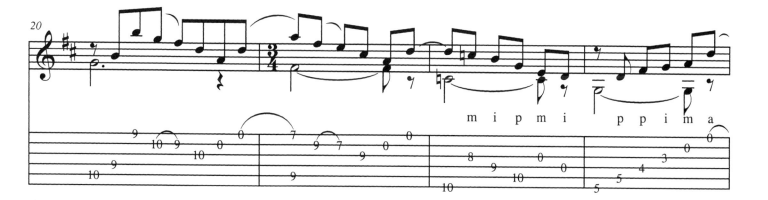

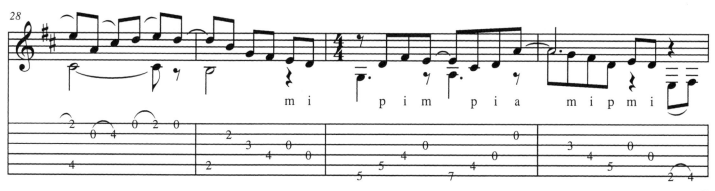

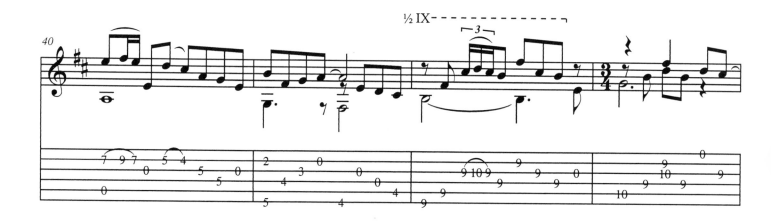

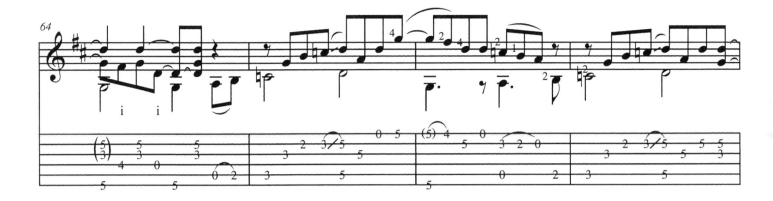

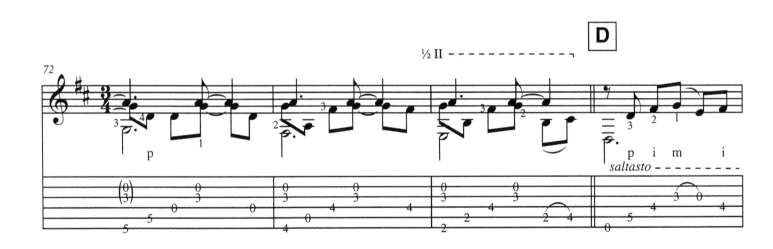

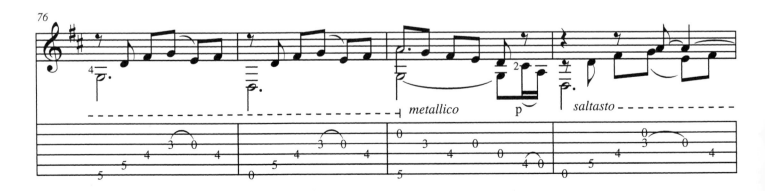

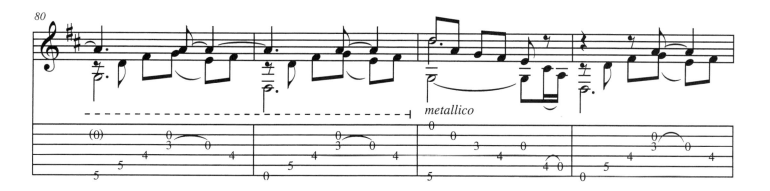

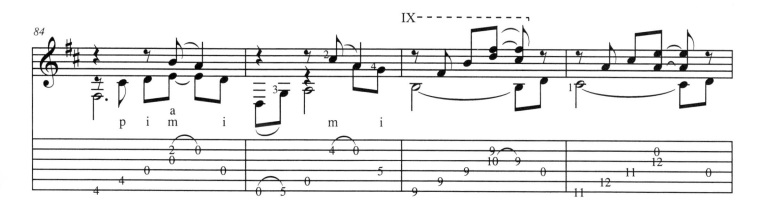

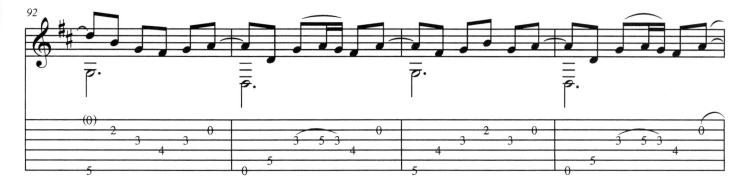

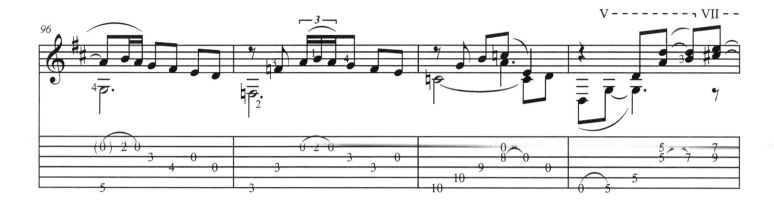

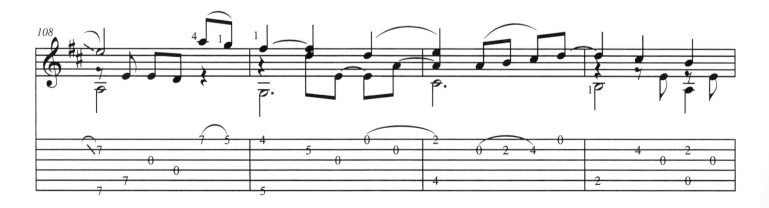

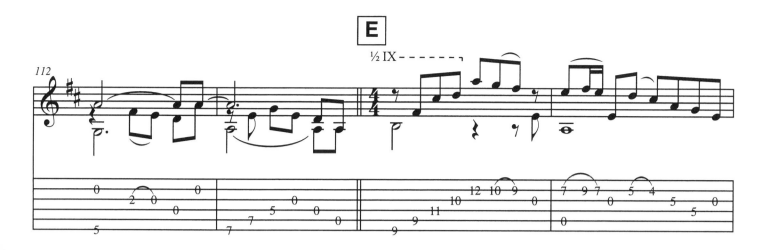

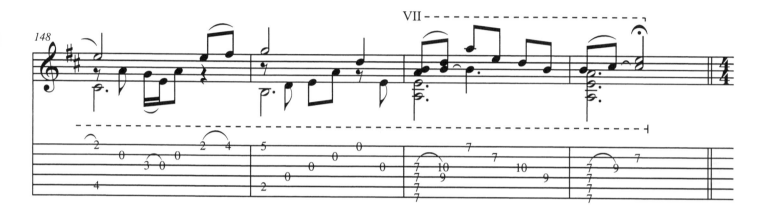

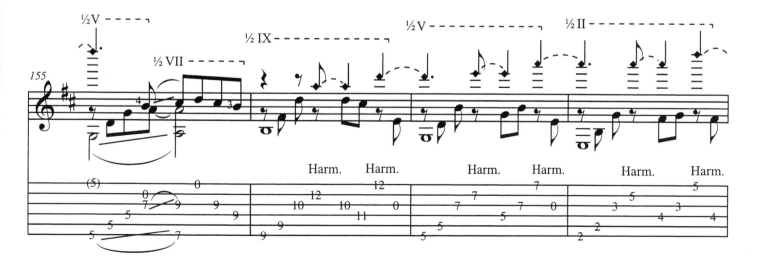

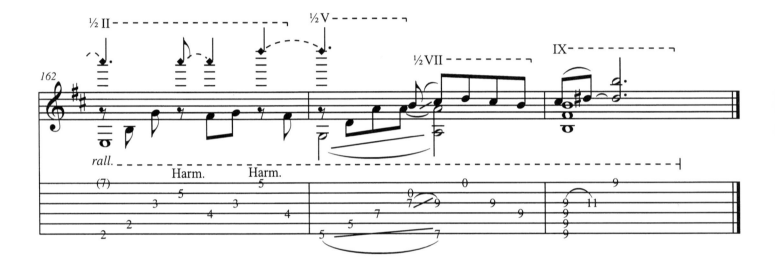

from *Deep at Night*

Blue Trout

By Alex de Grassi

Gtr. 1, Tuning: (low to high) D-A-D-G-A-D

*Slapped forcefully with side of right-hand
thumb, so that string sounds against the frets.

**As before

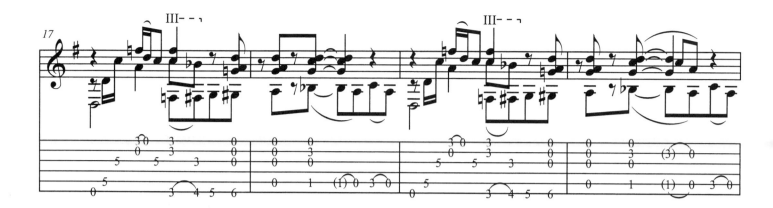

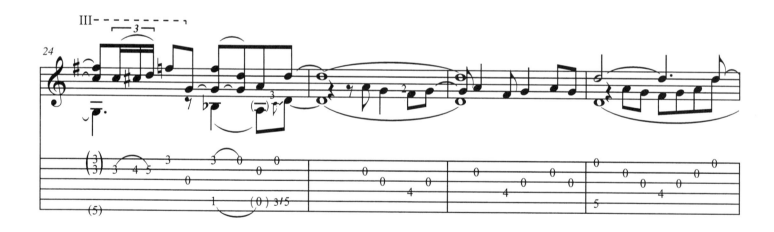

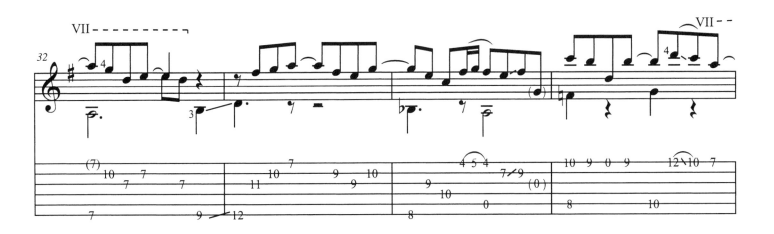

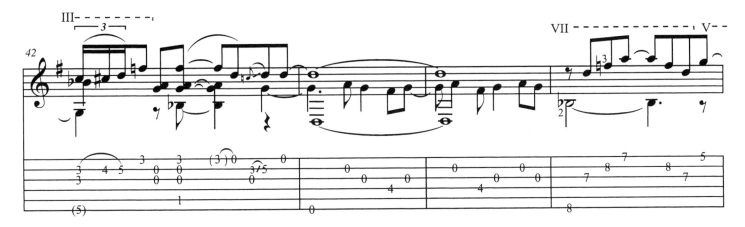

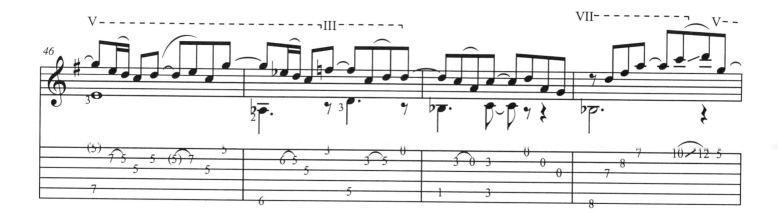

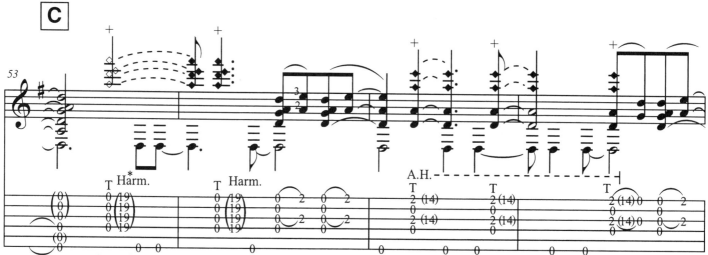

*Fret first number with left hand and slap w/ right hand across the fret indicated in parentheses.
Notes with two fret numbers (one in parentheses) create harmonics; notes with one number do
not create harmonics.

**In section C, all upstemmed notes are slapped with right-hand index finger; all downstemmed
notes are slapped with right-hand thumb. Other notes may sound.

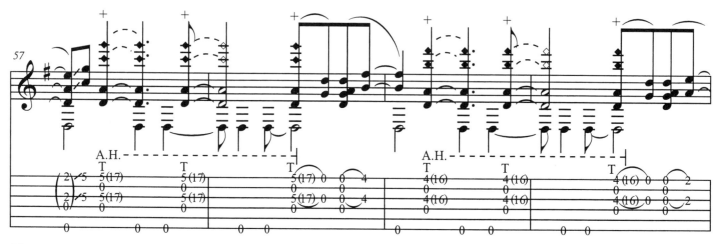

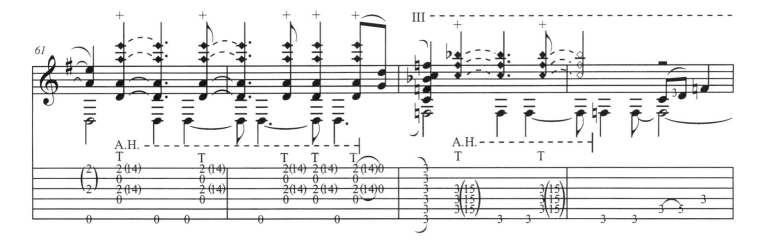

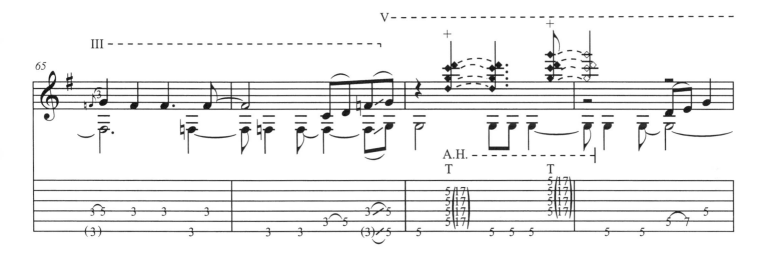

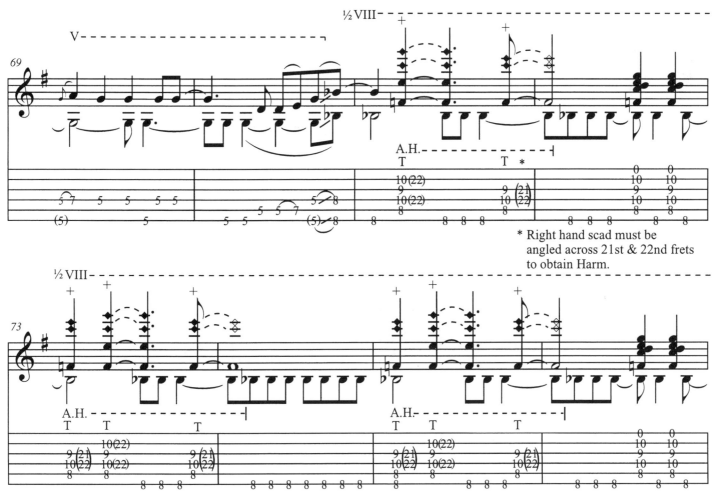

* Right hand scad must be
angled across 21st & 22nd frets
to obtain Harm.

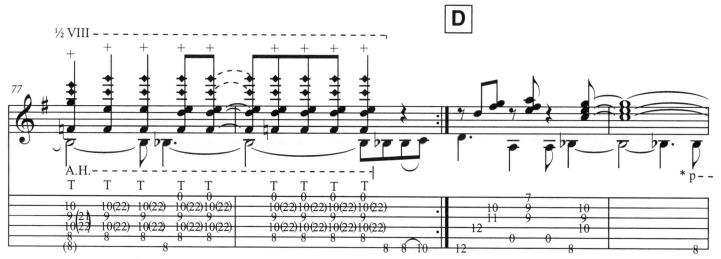

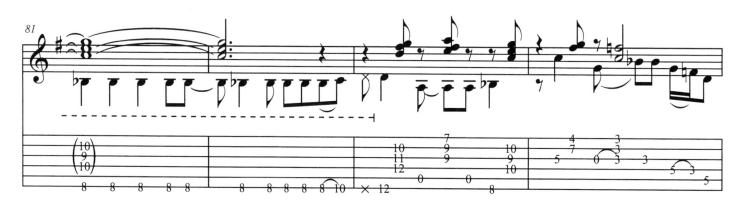

* Slapped forcefully with side of
right hand thumb, so that the string
sounds against the frets.

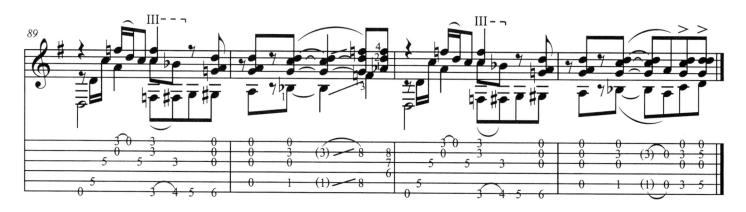

from *Deep at Night*

Bright Sky

By Alex de Grassi

Gtr. 1, Tuning: (low to high) E♭-G-D-G-B♭-D

Moderately ♩ = 98

Gtr. 1 (acous.)

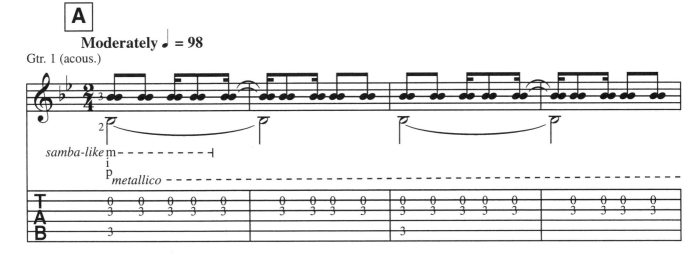

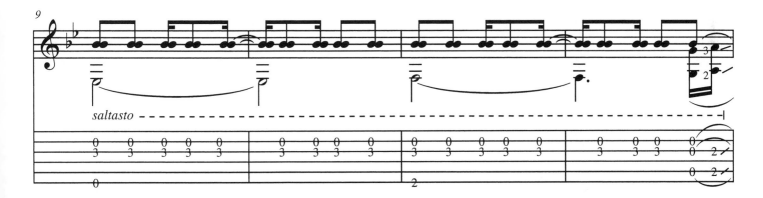

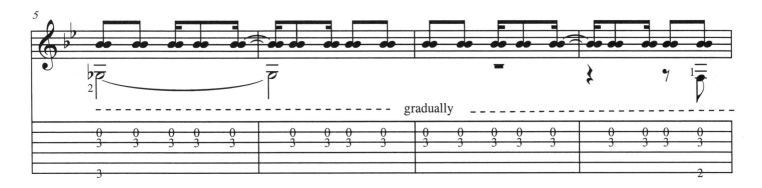

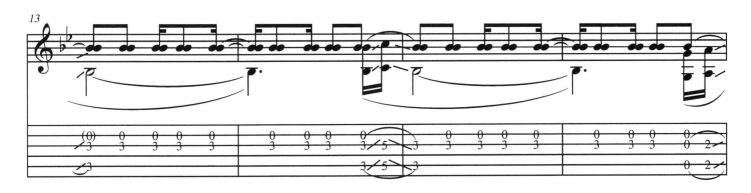

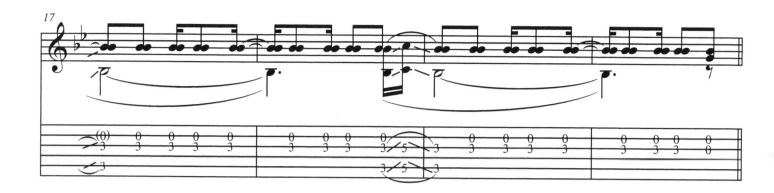

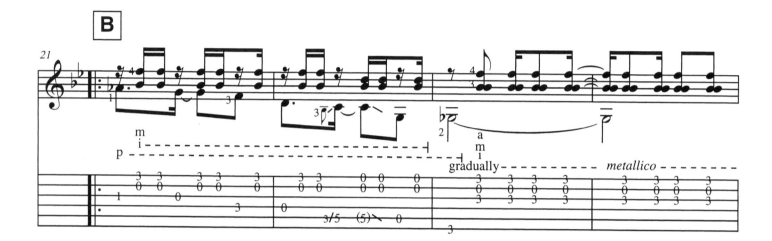

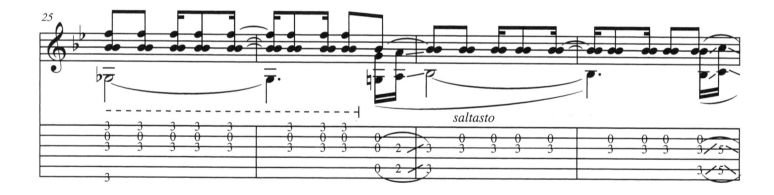

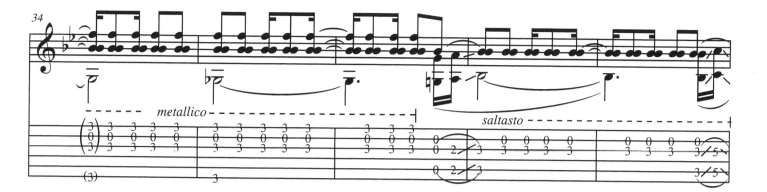

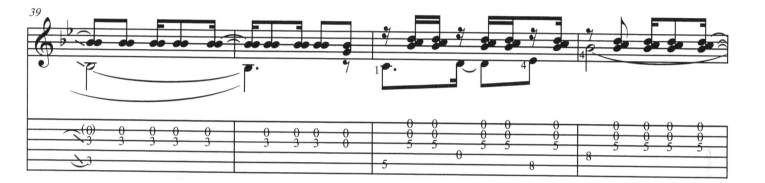

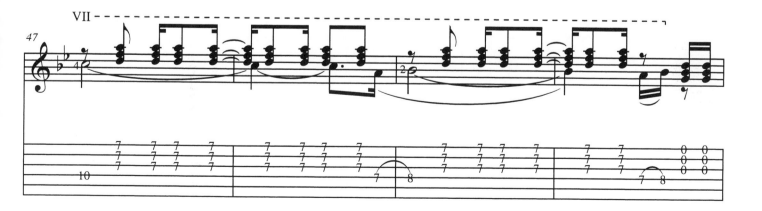

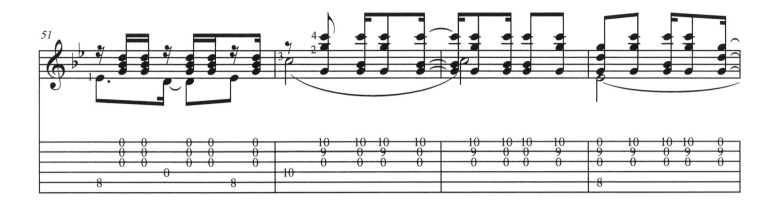

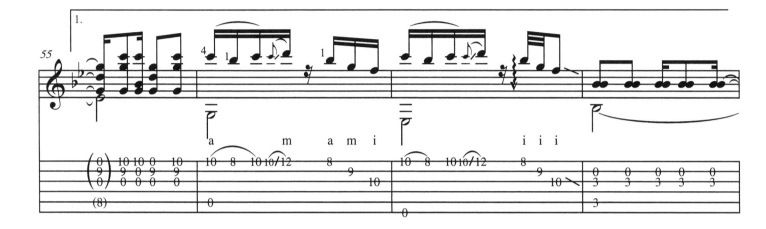

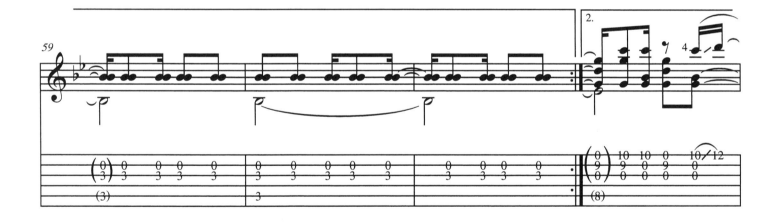

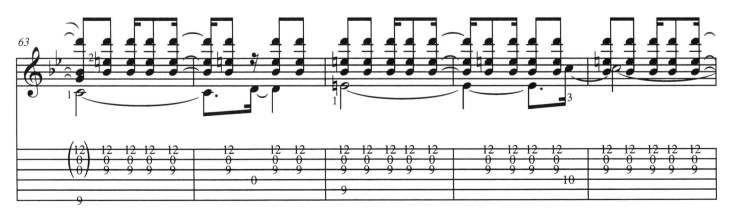

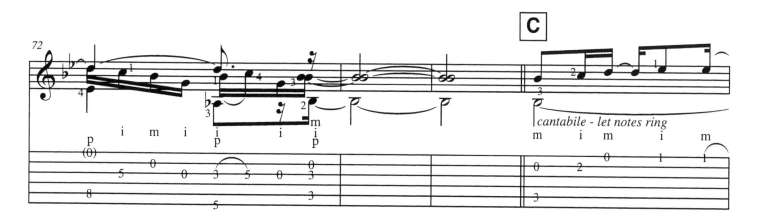

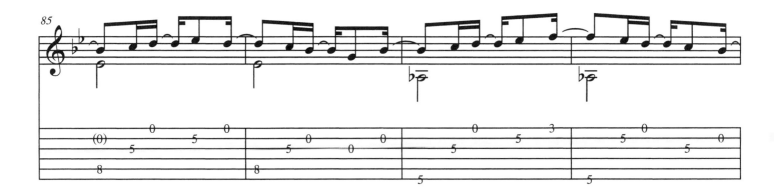

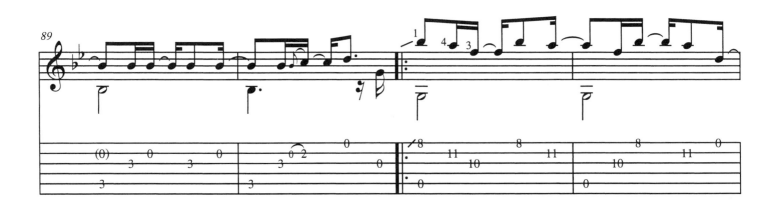

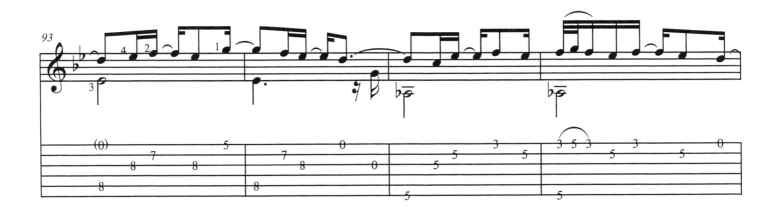

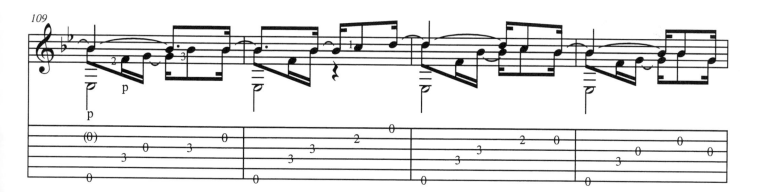

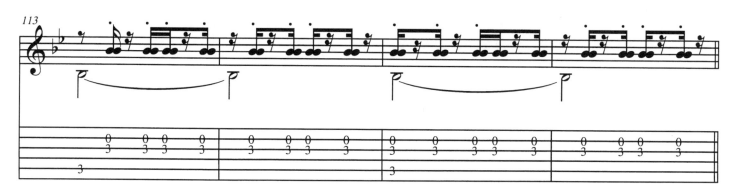

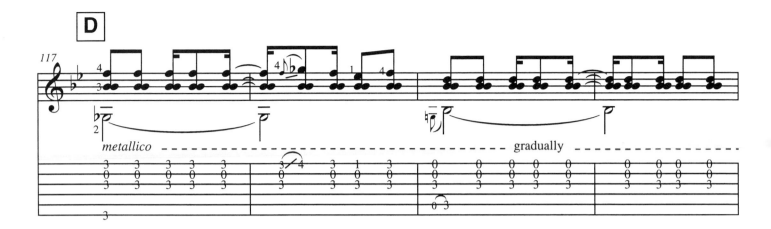

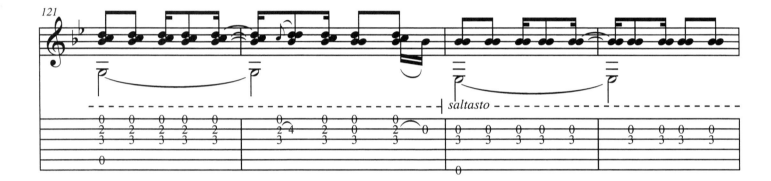

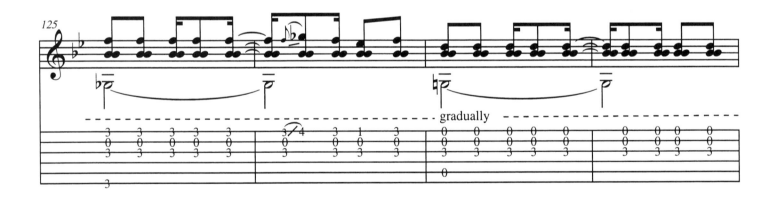

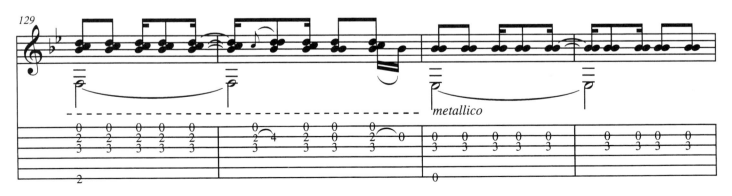

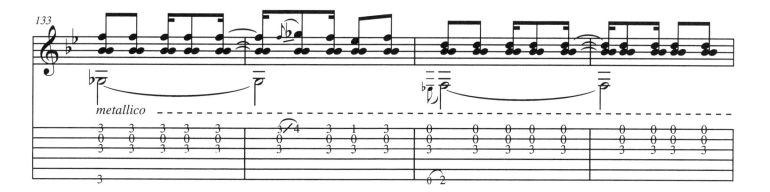

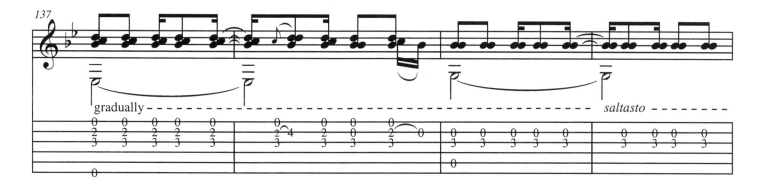

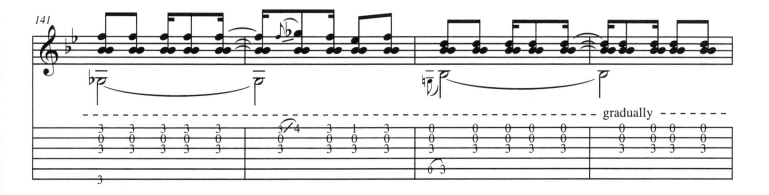

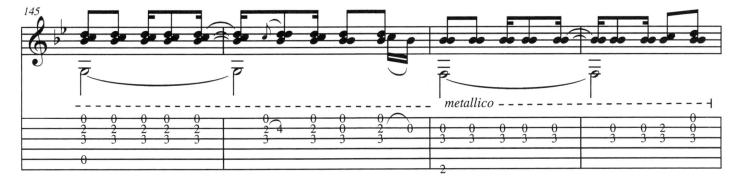

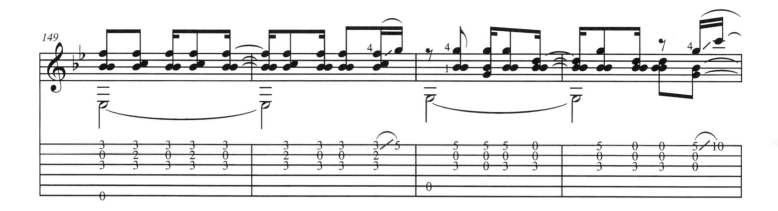

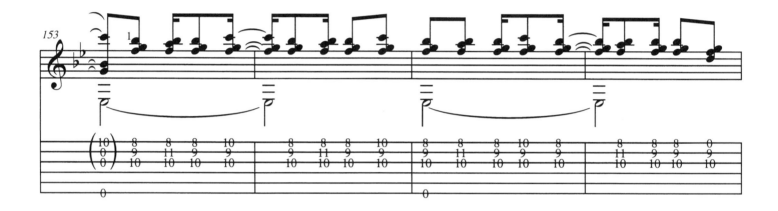

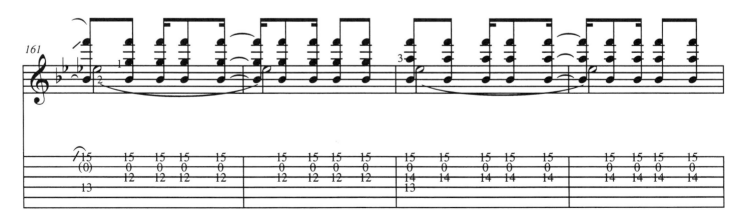

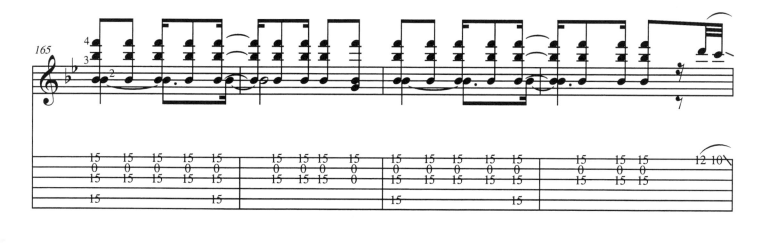

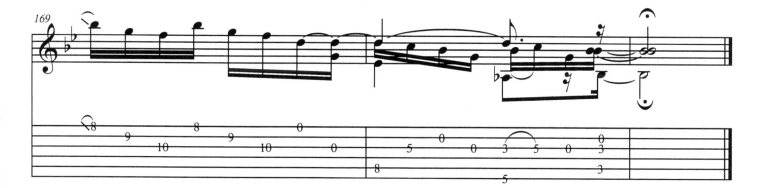

from *Southern Exposure*
Cumulus
By Alex de Grassi

Gtr. 1, Tuning: (low to high) D-A-D-G-B-E

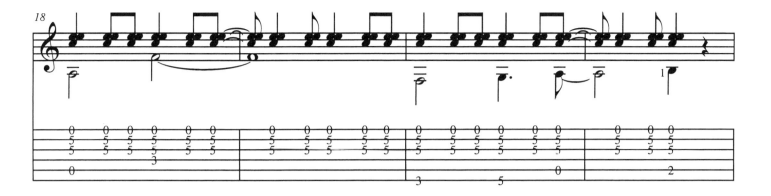

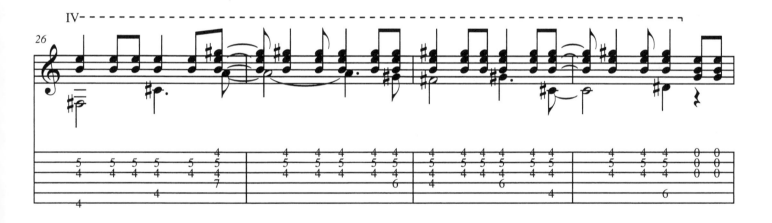

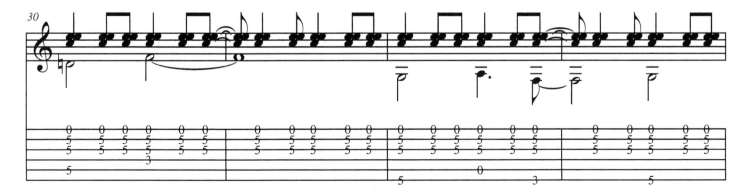

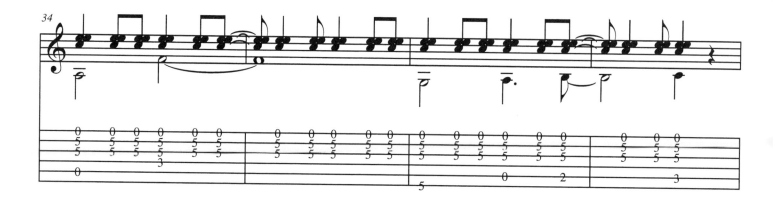

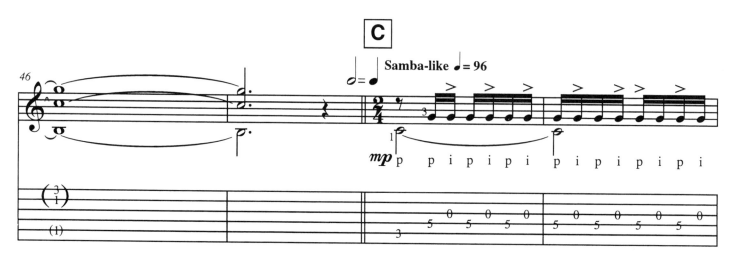

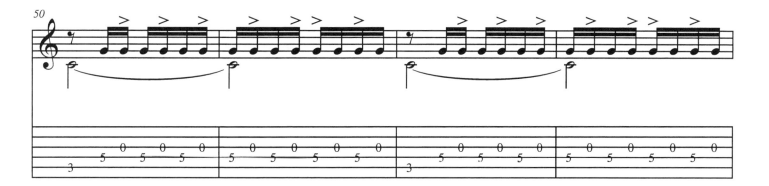

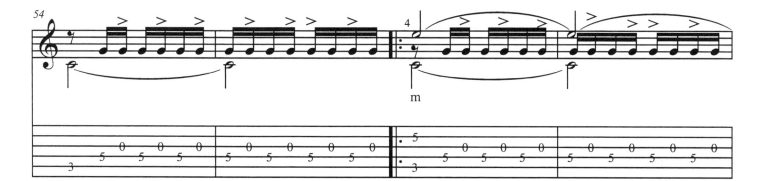

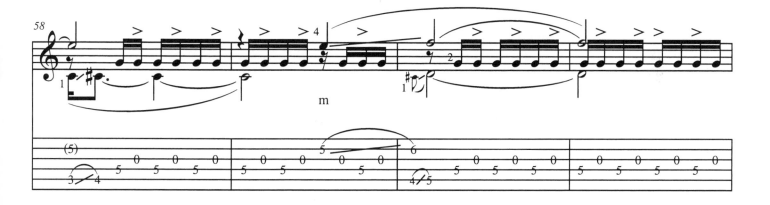

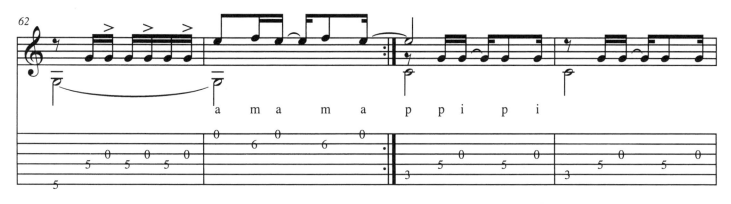

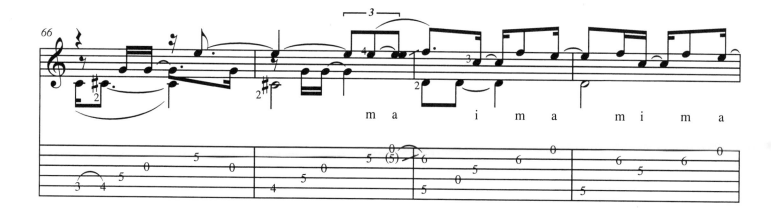

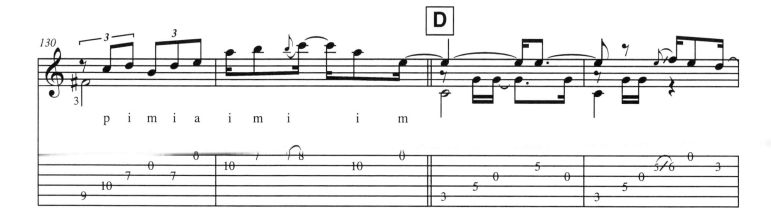

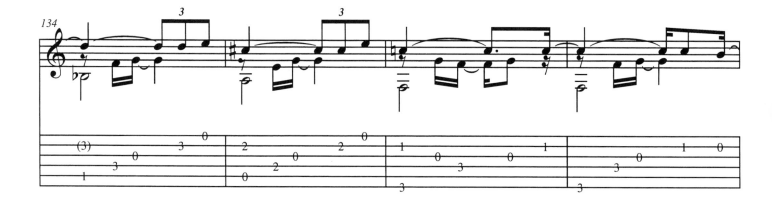

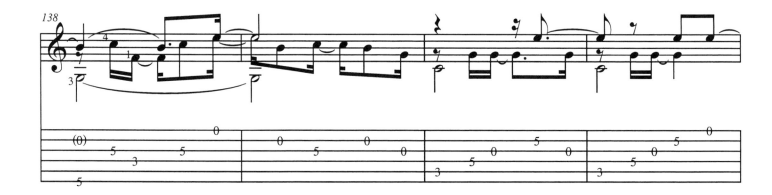

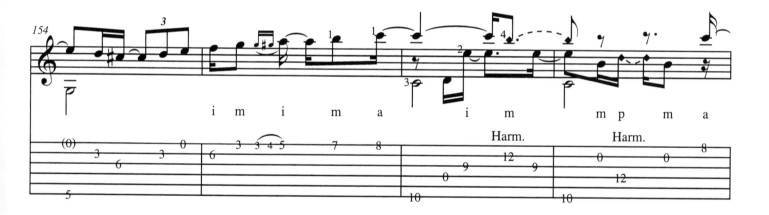

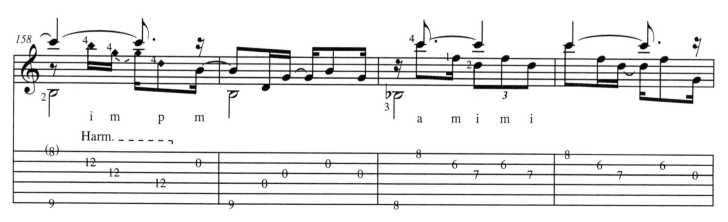

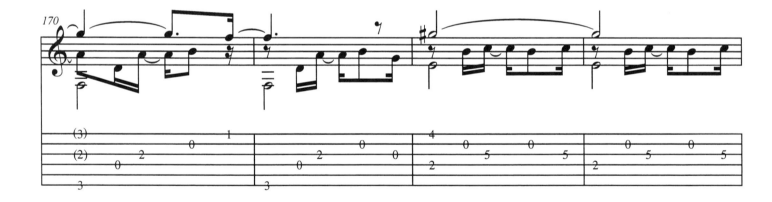

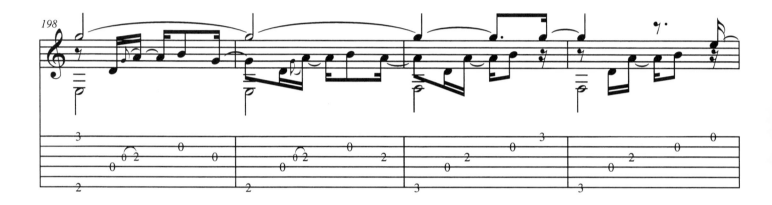

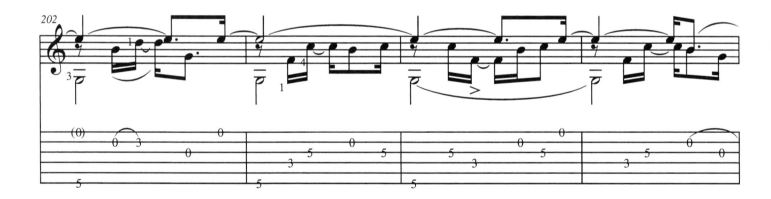

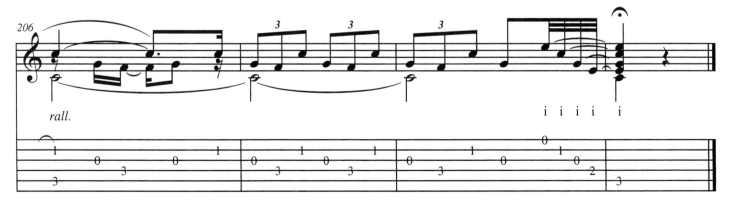

from *Deep at Night*

Deep at Night

By Alex de Grassi

Gtr. 1, Tuning: (low to high) E♭-G-D-G-B♭-D

*Slap downstemmed notes very softly with side of right-hand thumb very close to the bridge—almost over the saddle—to create a very soft, drum-like sound.

**Fret 4th and 5th strings at 7th and 8th frets with left hand;
lightly place right-hand index finger across 19th and 20th frets
while picking with right-hand ring finger across all 6 strings
(sixth string open).

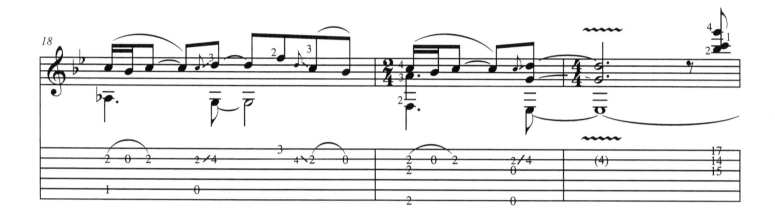

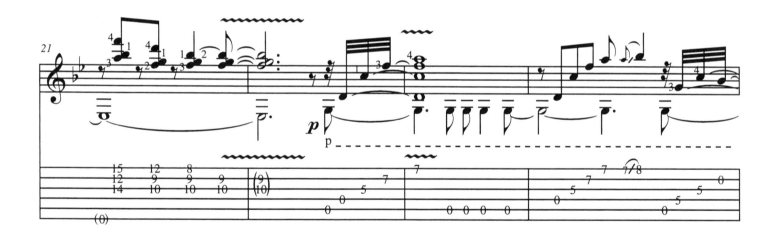

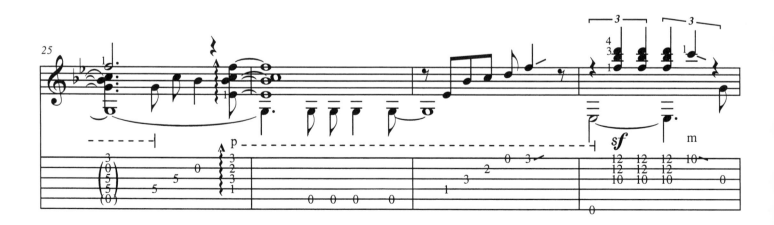

C

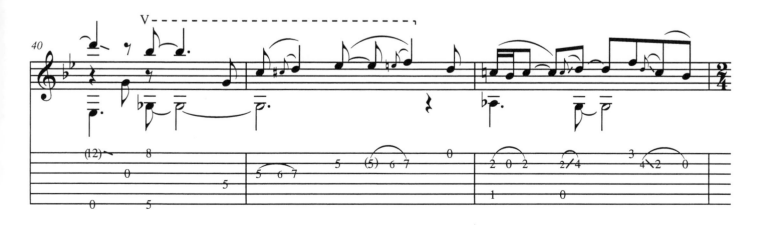

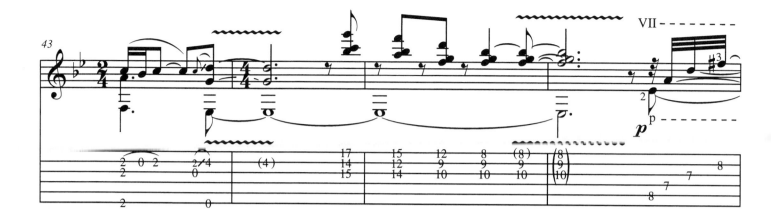

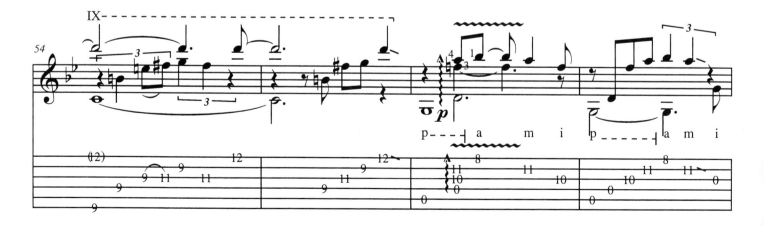

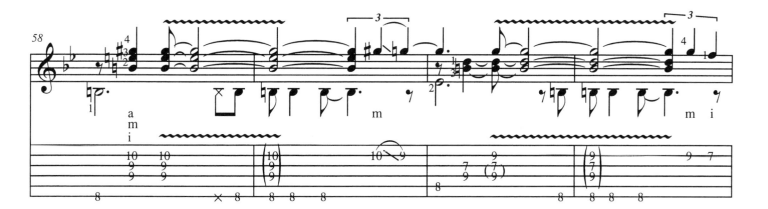

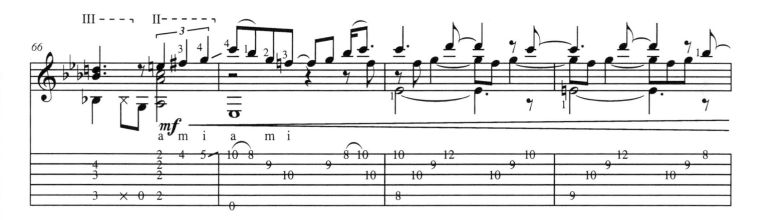

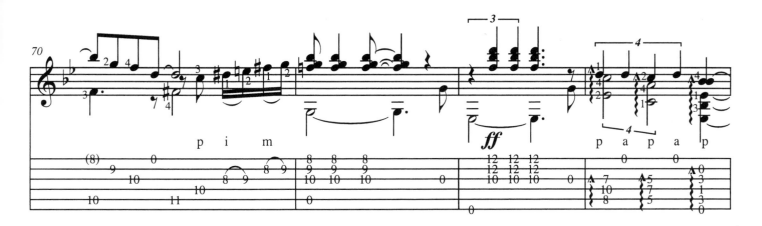

Vamp out

from *Slow Circle*

Klamath

By Alex de Grassi

Gtr. 1, Tuning: (low to high) D-A-D-F-G-C

Moderately fast ♩ = 144
Gtr. 1 (acous.)

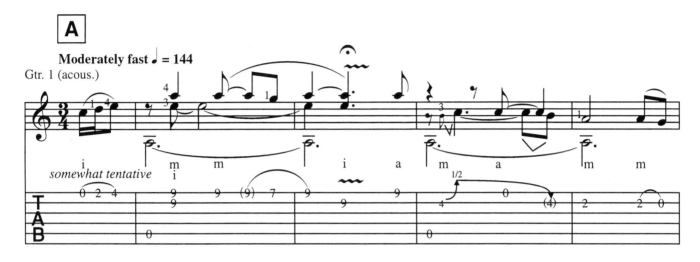

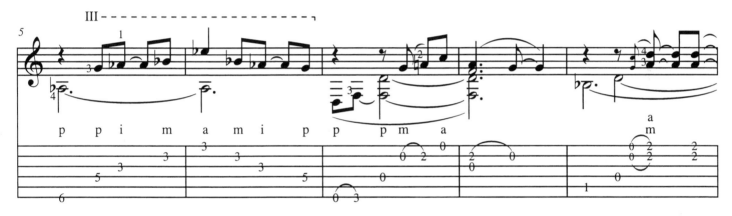

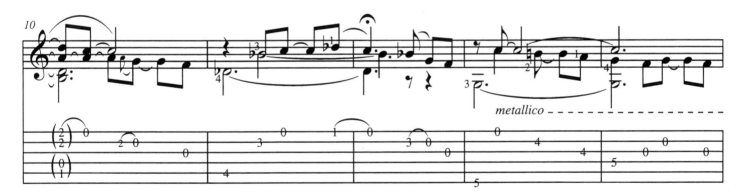

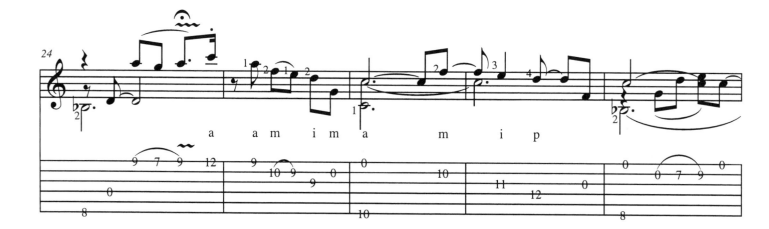

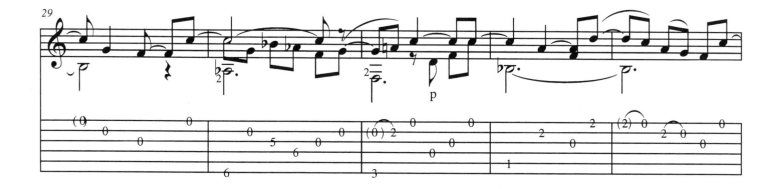

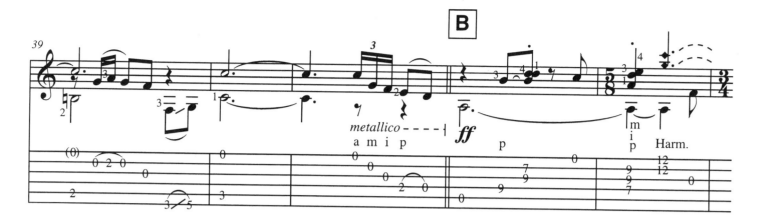

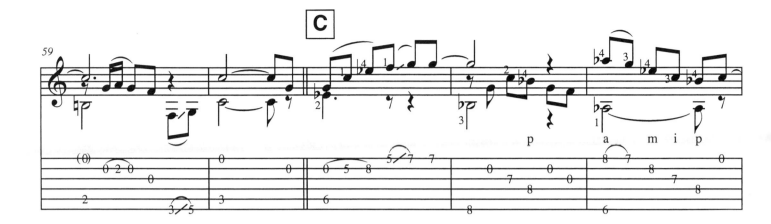

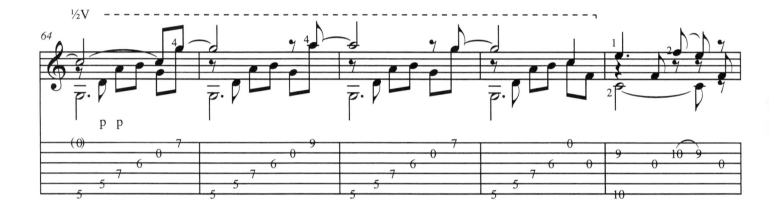

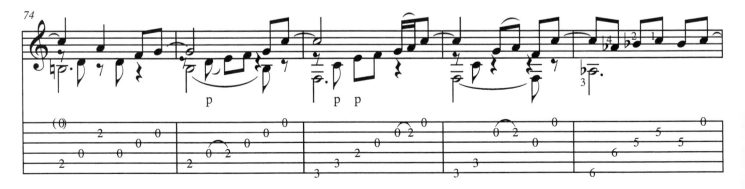

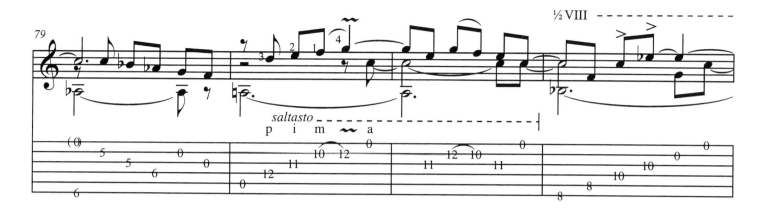

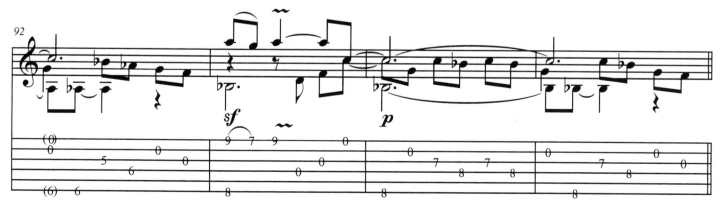

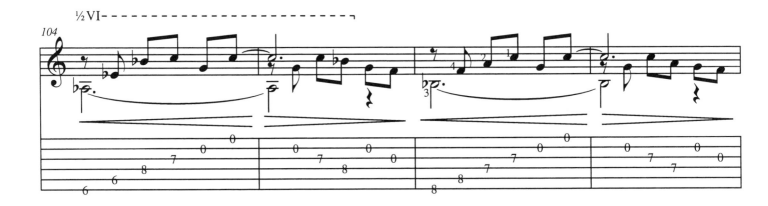

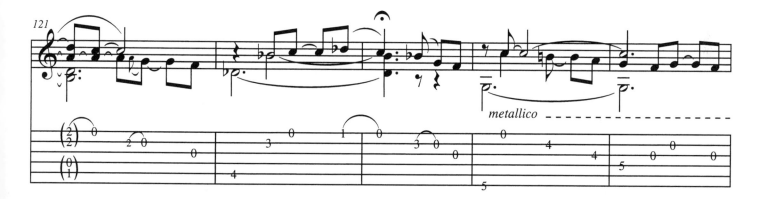

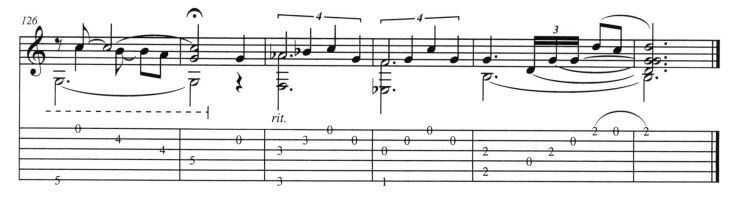

from *Deep at Night*

Short Order

By Alex de Grassi

Gtr. 1, Tuning: (low to high) D-A-D-G-A-D

Moderately fast ♩ = 168

Gtr. 1 (acous.)

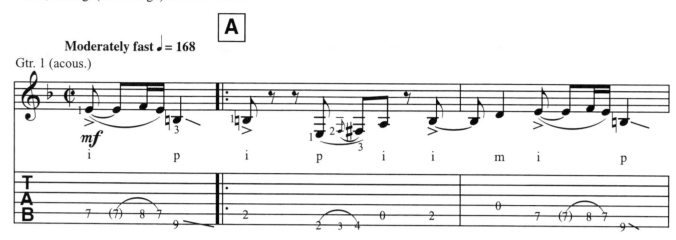

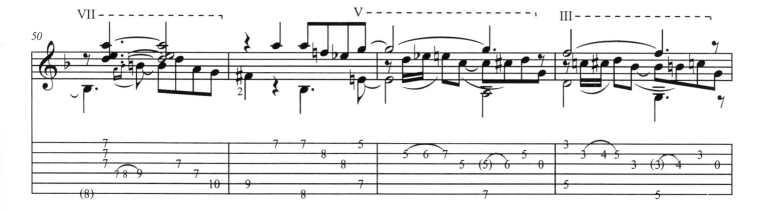

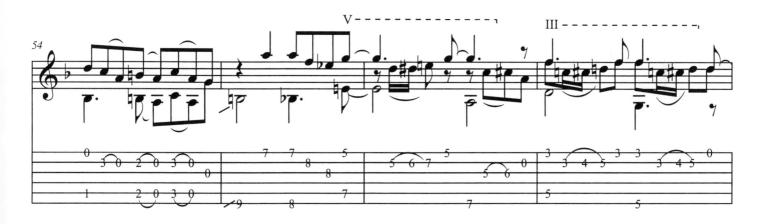

from *Slow Circle*
Sleeping Lady
By Alex de Grassi

Gtr. 1, Tuning: (low to high) D-A-D-E-A-C

A

Moderately fast ♩ = 138

Gtr. 1 (acous.)

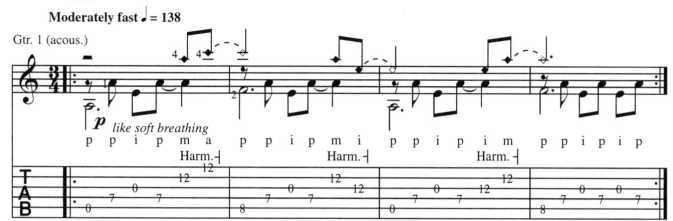

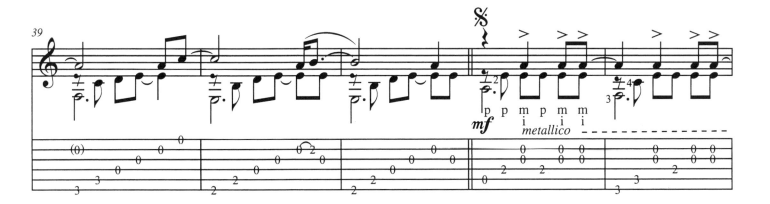

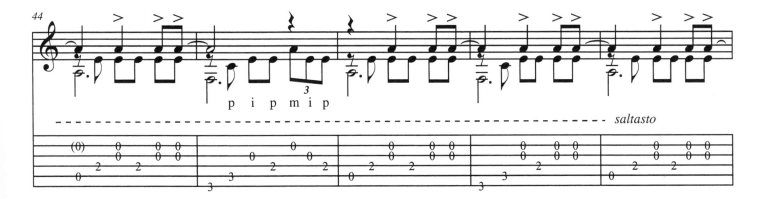

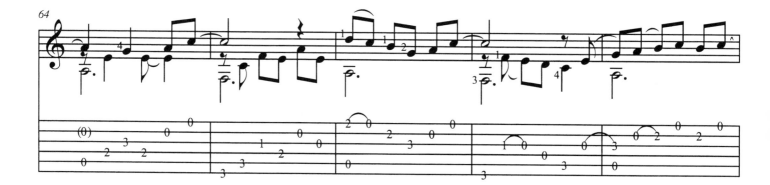

2nd time, To Coda

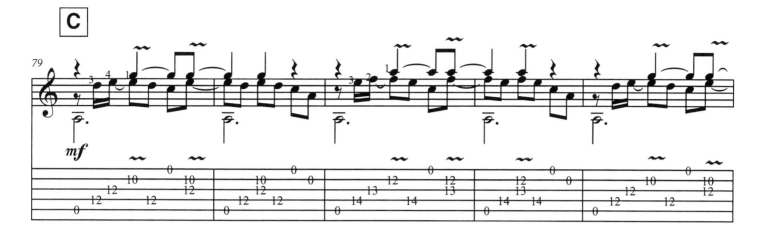

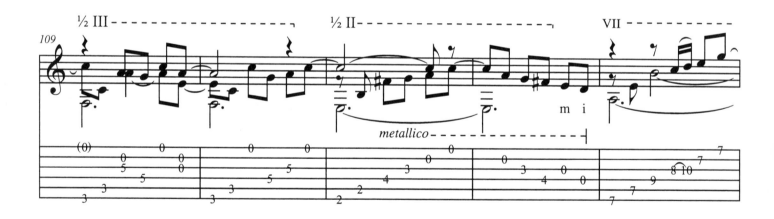

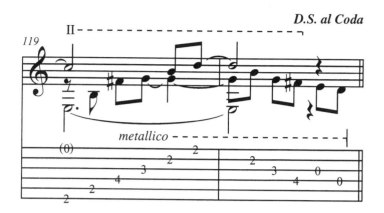

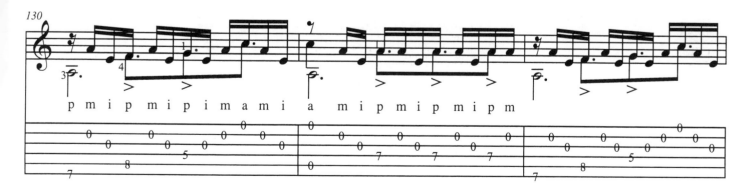

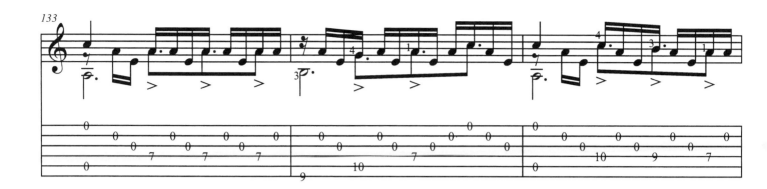

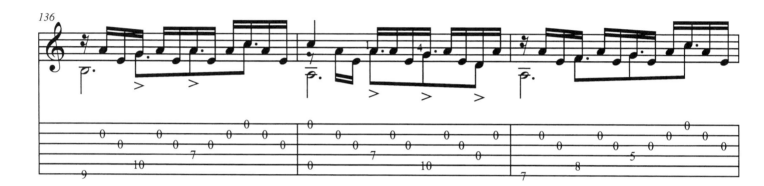

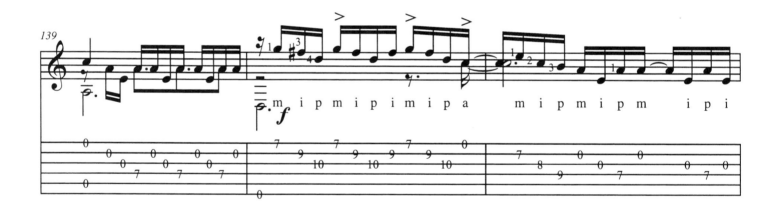

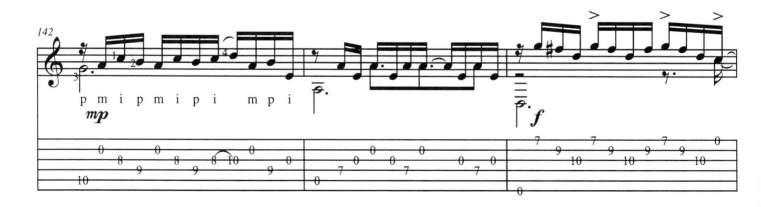

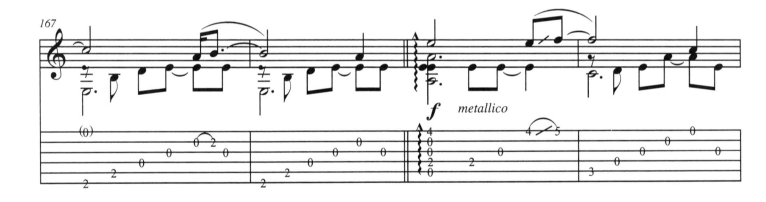

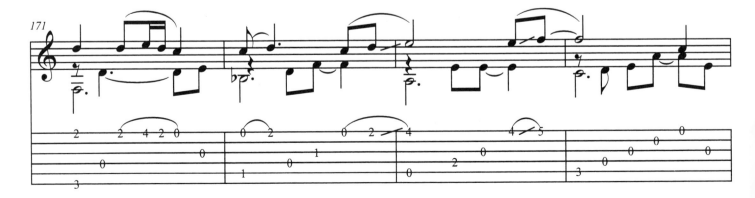

rit.

rall.   *poco a poco al fine*

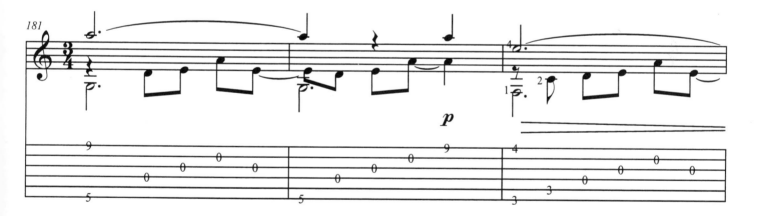

p

Turning: Turning Back

By Alex de Grassi

Gtr. 1, Tuning: (low to high) D-A-D-E-A-D

A

Moderato ♩ = 126

Gtr. 1 (acous.)

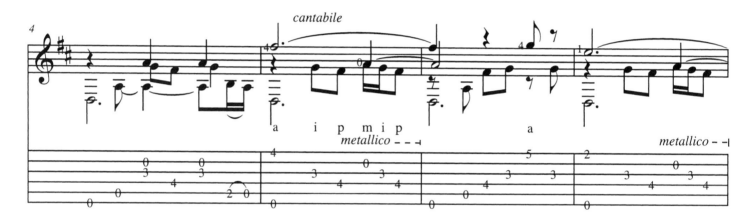

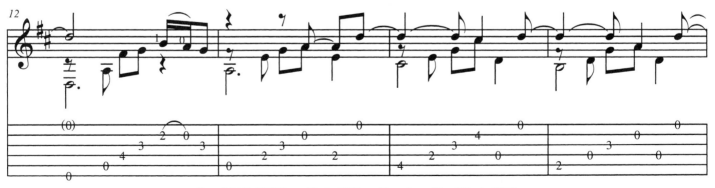

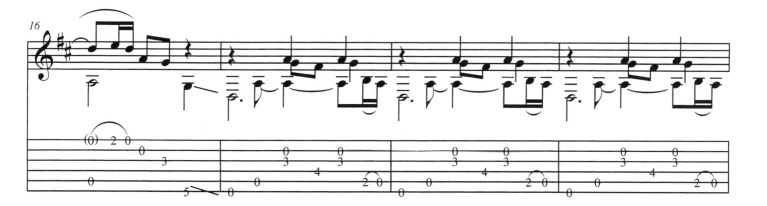

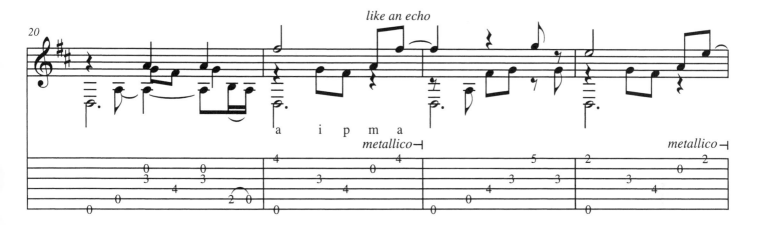

like an echo

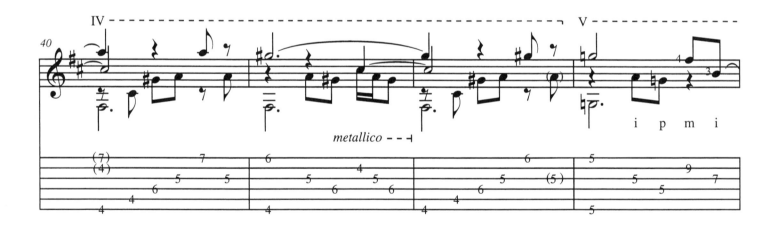

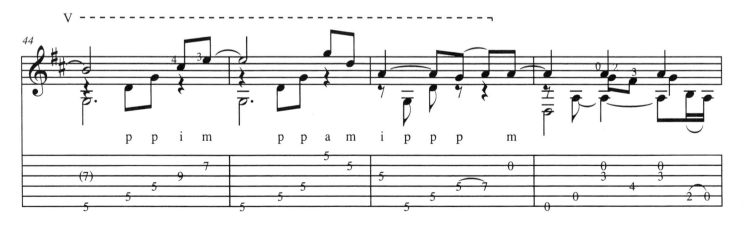

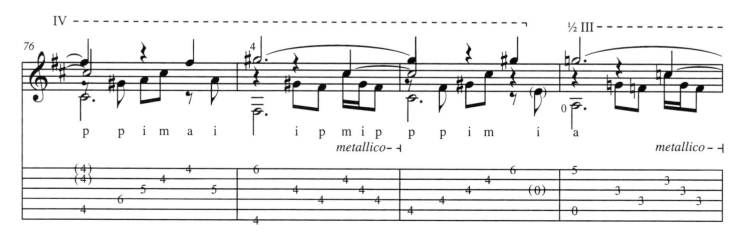

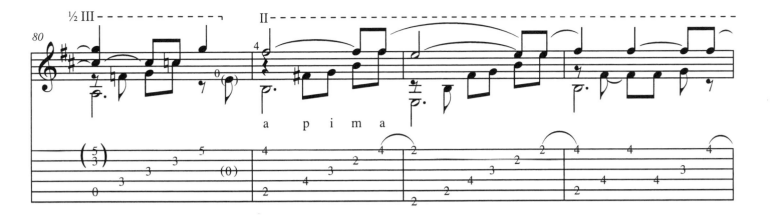

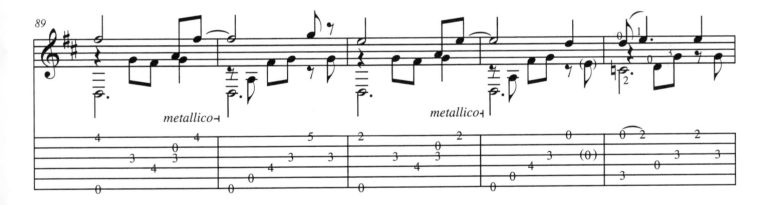

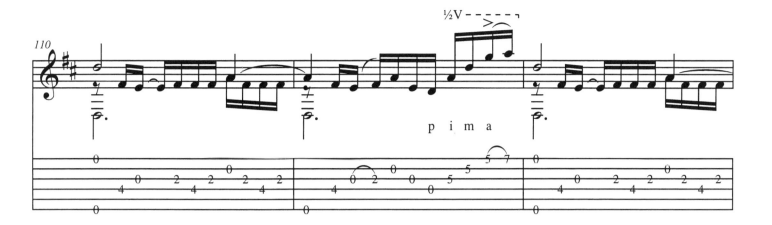

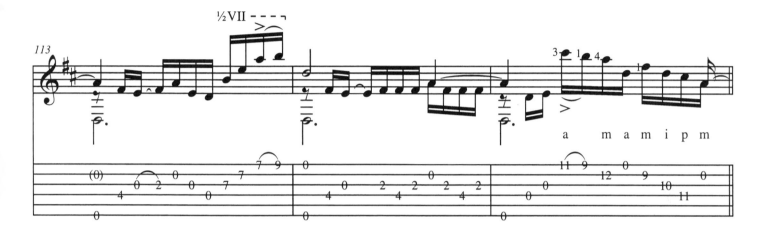

D

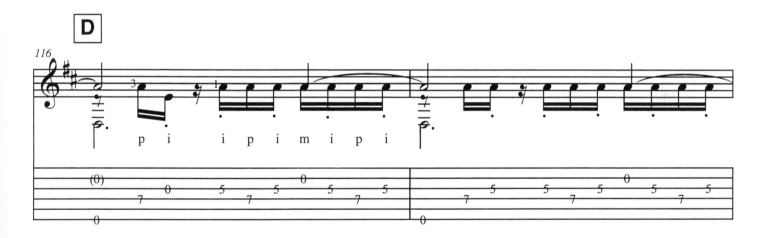

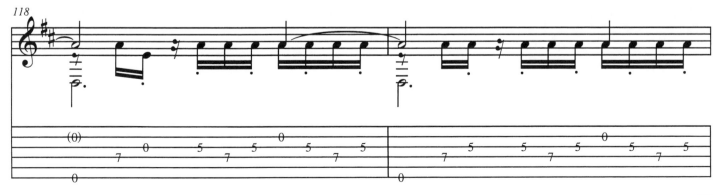

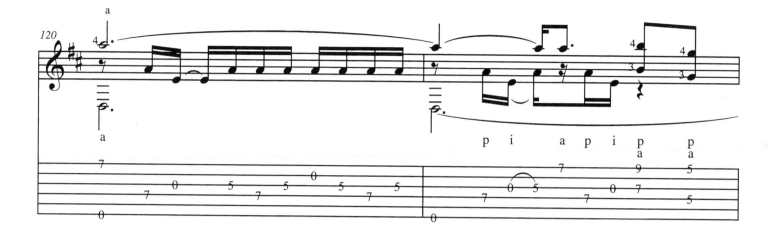

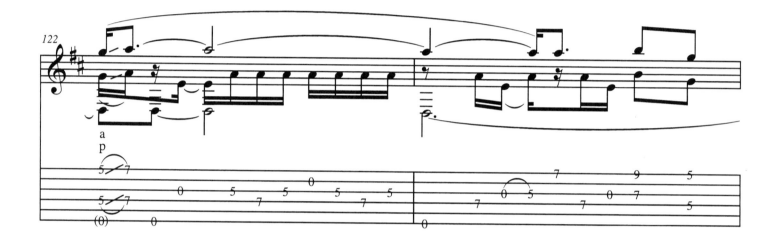

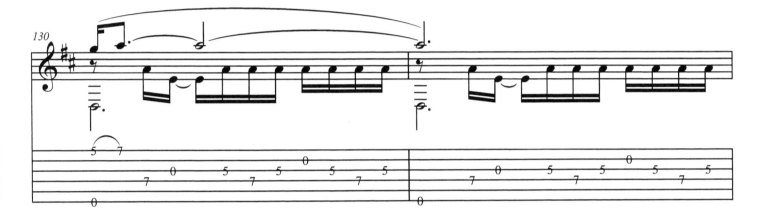

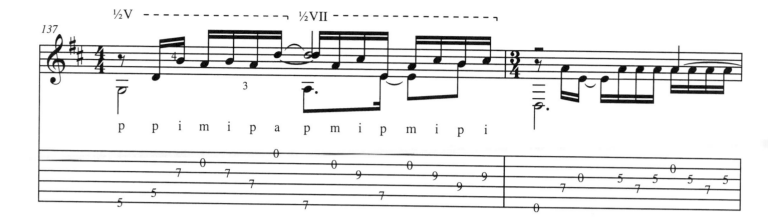

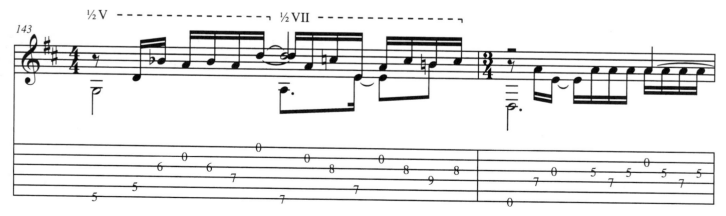

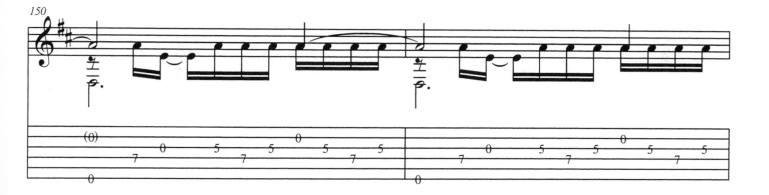

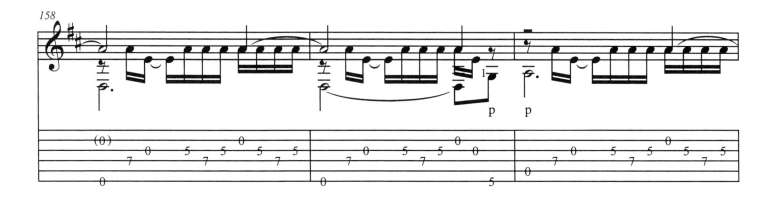

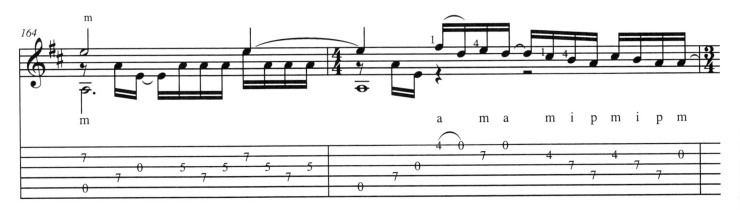

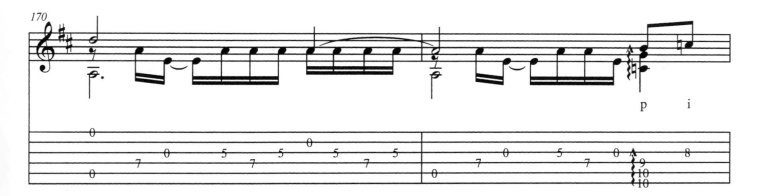

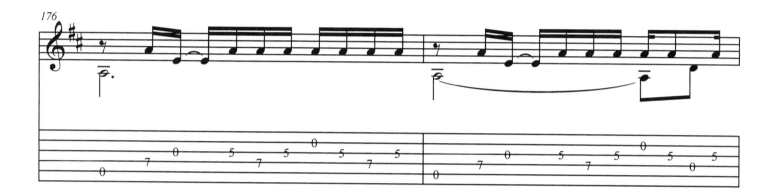

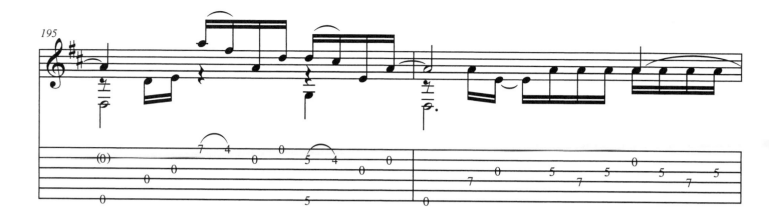

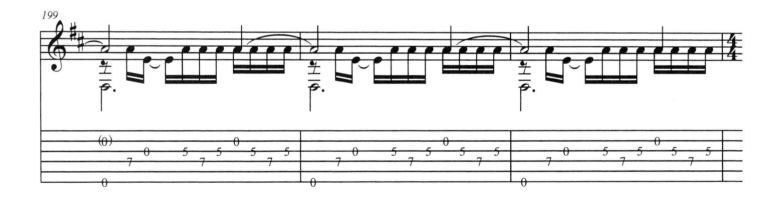

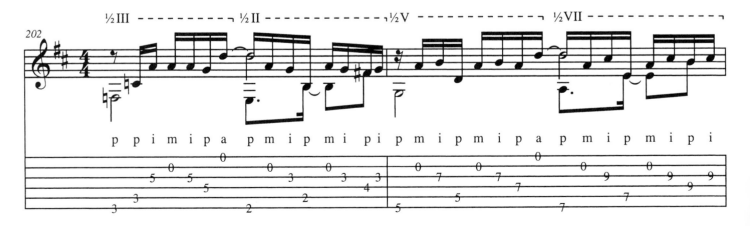

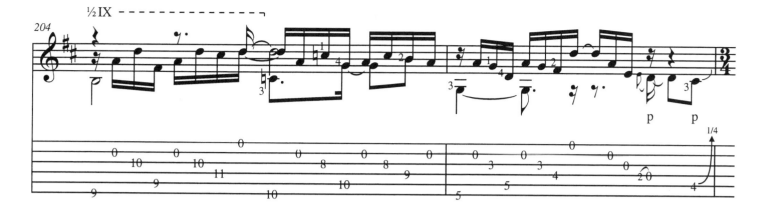

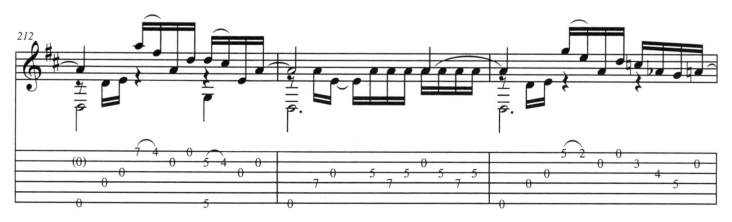

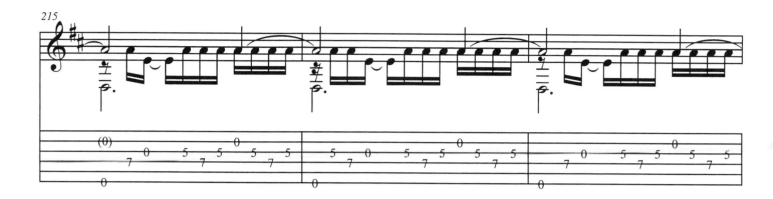

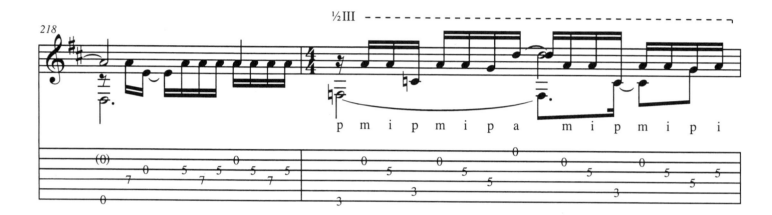

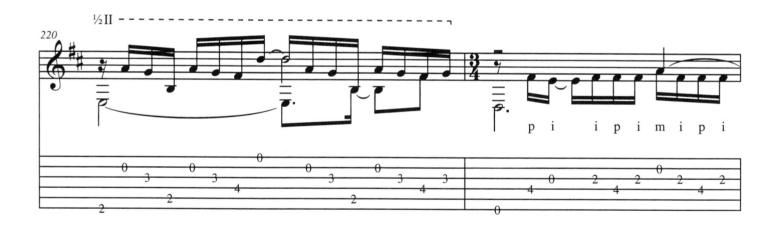

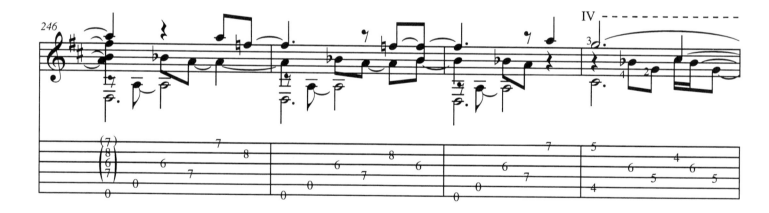

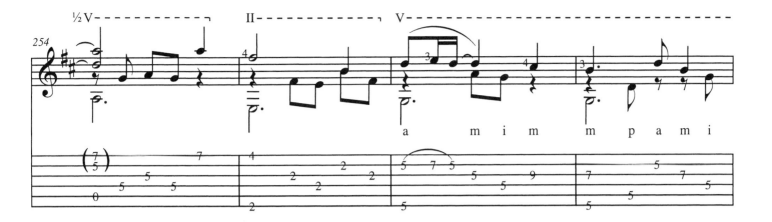

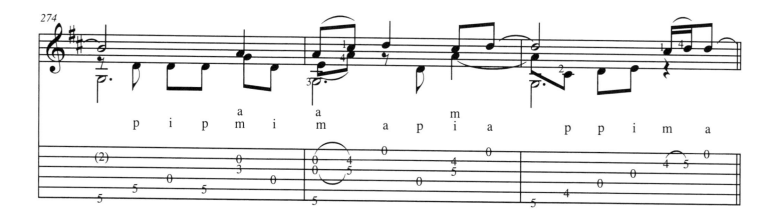

G

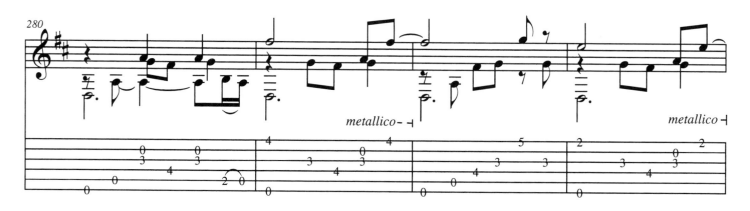

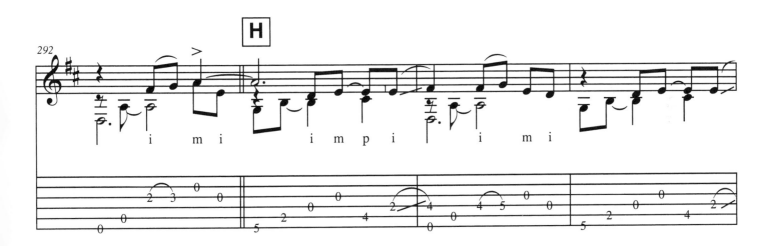

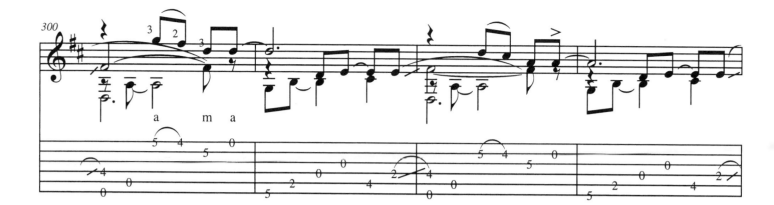

Guitar Notation Legend

Guitar music can be notated three different ways: on a *musical staff*, in *tablature*, and in *rhythm slashes*.

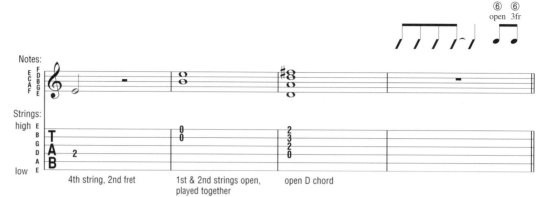

RHYTHM SLASHES are written above the staff. Strum chords in the rhythm indicated. Use the chord diagrams found at the top of the first page of the transcription for the appropriate chord voicings. Round noteheads indicate single notes.

THE MUSICAL STAFF shows pitches and rhythms and is divided by bar lines into measures. Pitches are named after the first seven letters of the alphabet.

TABLATURE graphically represents the guitar fingerboard. Each horizontal line represents a string, and each number represents a fret.

4th string, 2nd fret

1st & 2nd strings open, played together

open D chord

HALF-STEP BEND: Strike the note and bend up 1/2 step.

WHOLE-STEP BEND: Strike the note and bend up one step.

GRACE NOTE BEND: Strike the note and immediately bend up as indicated.

SLIGHT (MICROTONE) BEND: Strike the note and bend up 1/4 step.

BEND AND RELEASE: Strike the note and bend up as indicated, then release back to the original note. Only the first note is struck.

PRE-BEND: Bend the note as indicated, then strike it.

VIBRATO: The string is vibrated by rapidly bending and releasing the note with the fretting hand.

WIDE VIBRATO: The pitch is varied to a greater degree by vibrating with the fretting hand.

HAMMER-ON: Strike the first (lower) note with one finger, then sound the higher note (on the same string) with another finger by fretting it without picking.

PULL-OFF: Place both fingers on the notes to be sounded. Strike the first note and without picking, pull the finger off to sound the second (lower) note.

LEGATO SLIDE: Strike the first note and then slide the same fret-hand finger up or down to the second note. The second note is not struck.

SHIFT SLIDE: Same as legato slide, except the second note is struck.

TRILL: Very rapidly alternate between the notes indicated by continuously hammering on and pulling off.

TAPPING: Hammer ("tap") the fret indicated with the pick-hand index or middle finger and pull off to the note fretted by the fret hand.

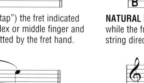

NATURAL HARMONIC: Strike the note while the fret-hand lightly touches the string directly over the fret indicated.

PINCH HARMONIC: The note is fretted normally and a harmonic is produced by adding the edge of the thumb or the tip of the index finger of the pick hand to the normal pick attack.

PICK SCRAPE: The edge of the pick is rubbed down (or up) the string, producing a scratchy sound.

MUFFLED STRINGS: A percussive sound is produced by laying the fret hand across the string(s) without depressing, and striking them with the pick hand.

PALM MUTING: The note is partially muted by the pick hand lightly touching the string(s) just before the bridge.

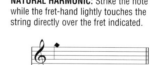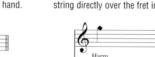

RAKE: Drag the pick across the strings indicated with a single motion.

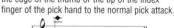

TREMOLO PICKING: The note is picked as rapidly and continuously as possible.

VIBRATO BAR DIVE AND RETURN: The pitch of the note or chord is dropped a specified number of steps (in rhythm), then returned to the original pitch.

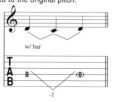

VIBRATO BAR SCOOP: Depress the bar just before striking the note, then quickly release the bar.

VIBRATO BAR DIP: Strike the note and then immediately drop a specified number of steps, then release back to the original pitch.